**Extraordinary Living: Volume I
A Testimonial & Devotional**

By Shana Underwood-Stephens
Edited by *Diamond Mind Book Editors (2023)*

Table of Contents

Chapter 1............*Inspiration*
Chapter 2.........*The Power of Your Vision*
Chapter 3......*The Gift That Keeps on Giving*
Chapter 4...............*The Prophesy*
Chapter 5.................*Success v. Failure*
Chapter 6 ....*Childish Things*
Chapter 7..................*Extraordinary Living*
Chapter 8 ....*If Not You, Then Who?*
Chapter 9 ....*Soul Ties*
Chapter 10 ....*The Wilderness*
Chapter 11 ....*Obedience*
Chapter 12..................*Reflections*

Dedication

This book is dedicated to all creative souls who may be thinking that their time has passed. You are not too old. You are not insignificant. You are seasoned and ready to be used more than ever before.

Go for your passion wholeheartedly. Believe in yourself even when no one else does. Make a habit of learning new things so that you never have to accept no for an answer. You can always do it yourself.

Chapter 1
Inspiration

This testimonial was not written because I wanted to write a book. It was written after constant urging from other men and women of God who proclaimed that I was supposed to be writing a book. Some of them were meeting me for the first time. Others had known me all my life and followed me on social media. A few were students in my classrooms. I, however, felt that my life was too ordinary to write an interesting book. I thought good books were written by people whose lives started out traumatically and ended triumphantly.

Although my life did start out humbly, it was a relatively happy life with loving people around me. So, why would God want me to tell people about it? Because I decided to be obedient in January of 2023, I decided not to ignore the Holy Spirit. I decided to wholeheartedly do what God was telling me to do. So, I took the first few months of the year to write down a few testimonies that I was already sharing with others over and over again. I took the most inspiring stories from different stages of my life and shared them the same way I'd done for years. So, here it is - finished. I hope this testimonial is as edifying to read as it was to write.

Before we go any further:
Do you have any *unfinished* assignments that God has instructed you to complete? If so, tell me about one.

Chapter 2

The Power of Your Vision

Never be afraid to dream big. When you envision something for your life, don't take it lightly. Tap into the vision and know that it's God's way of revealing what your future can potentially be. If it were not possible, He would not allow you to see it. We must be able to see beyond our present circumstances to change them. When we experience revelations of our own future or the future of someone we love, we should not only write them down, but write down the necessary steps for making it a reality. Work toward each step. Then, check them off as we accomplish them. Keep God in the forefront so that you will be confident that you are under His direction. Trust that if you follow His lead, He will open up doors and attract the people who will assist you toward your vision, as you also work towards it.

I have been fortunate to have many mother-figures in my life, some which will be mentioned throughout this book. Two of them were visionaries in my life - My birth mother and my Godmother (my high school drill team coach.) They were both instrumental in shaping me into a winner, and God knew that I needed both - not only for their guidance and protection, but also for their <u>visions</u>. I needed them both to reach my full potential.

My mother gave birth to me at age 16 in 1978. I grew up in a remote town in Georgia with a population that has fluctuated between 500-800 people throughout my lifetime.
Everybody knew everybody, and opportunities for prosperity and notoriety were far and few in between. Growing up, I rarely even traveled to Atlanta, which was only a 90-minute drive. Back then, Atlanta was not the mecca that it is today. However, I did witness its emergence as the music industry capital while I was in middle school and high school.
I wanted so much to be there, to be a part of it all. I was obsessed with the idea, and for me, this desire was related solely to Black music. Yet, Atlanta felt like it was on another continent to me. That's just how underprivileged we were and how unconnected we felt to people who thrived there.

So, this is where the visionaries made the difference. My birth mother had always dreamed bigger than Wilkinson County. She'd lived there all her life because she had started her family very young. Therefore, she desperately needed the support system that was established there. We were surrounded by aunts, uncles, grandparents, great-grandparents, great aunts and great uncles, and too many cousins to try to count. So, it was beautiful in that aspect. The downside was that the family had not ventured out much. Most of our elders had no college education, and our financial literacy was stunted by a lack of resources and information.

This, however, didn't stop my mother from wanting more for me and being willing to create avenues, invest money, and coach me herself to make things happen. She believed in me as a student. She believed in me as a performer, and it showed. She put me in pageants, helped me study for spelling bees (which I won year after year), wrote skits for me to perform at church so that I could sing for everybody.

  She didn't have much to work with as far as venues, but she knew that my talents were worth sharing. So, she did what she could, which was more than many others were doing at the time.

Church was my training ground for everything I was good at. She envisioned me doing something significant through education and entertainment well before I ever knew what I could be. She had a vision of me making it beyond the confines of small-town life, using my gifts to take me places. One thing was for sure, she didn't want me to sell myself short in life by making bad decisions.

In the spring of 1992, I was a happy 8th-grader with ambitions of trying out for the Varsity football cheerleading team at Wilco High for the next season. I had a decent cheerleading background, so I never imagined that I would not make the team. My cousin and I tried out together because we did everything together. At the end of the week, the new roster was posted, and sadly, I did not make the team. But what made it worse was the fact that my cousin did.

I felt so hurt and rejected that I don't think my cousin felt good at all about making the team. She and my mother spent the entire evening consoling me as I cried and cried over my failure. It would be the first time that my cousin and I were not on the same team or involved in the same activity at the same time. For years, my mother had consciously kept us busy doing things as a duo.

Fast forward a week later. I've had time to process my dejection and re-focus on enjoying the remainder of my 8th-grade year. While sitting in Mrs. Mason's math class engaged with a group of my peers, I remember hearing a knock at the door. A vaguely familiar woman asked to see me. Then, she asked to see my good buddy, Heather, after me. So, I went first.

When I stepped into the hallway, she introduced herself as Mrs. Hinton. She told me she was going to sponsor a new high school organization called a drill team/dance team. I was not familiar with drill teams but with majorettes. So, I grasped the concept. The organization was founded by a young girl only one year older than me, Jennifer Sanders. Mrs. Hinton explained that next year, she would be its official adult sponsor.

I wasn't sure how this applied to me, but what she said next changed my life. She said, "I was a judge at the cheerleading tryouts last week, and I want you to be on my dance team next year." It's hard to describe the way I felt at that moment, but it was redemptive to say the least. I felt shocked and vindicated all at once.

Dancing with the band seemed like much more fun than being a cheerleader. It was a new venture in my community, and I was going to be a part of it. The team would be small, only six members, but she had a *vision*. She promised that we were going to do some big things and boy did we do some BIG things.

She called my mother that evening to discuss her plans for the team, and my mother was on board immediately. I must say that I have never known my mother to trust another person with me so wholeheartedly. Yet, this white woman had my mother's trust from the very start.

Before I entered 9th grade, we went to summer dance camp at Georgia College in Milledgeville, Georgia. So, Mrs. Hinton exposed me to college campus life for the first time. We learned multiple field routines that week, and I was a bit overwhelmed. Fortunately, we went back to Wilkinson County and practiced them until we knew them like the backs of our hands. Once I made it through that experience, I fell in love with being a dancer. From there, we performed the halftime show of every Wilkinson County football game of the season and competed in countless band and drill team competitions all over the state. We worked very, very hard. On top of that, Mrs. Hinton was always instilling self-pride and school pride in us. She was constantly pushing us to be synchronized, professional, and prepared. She was tough and thoroughly bred. She was no-nonsense when it came to representing our school and ourselves to the best of our abilities.

She would take small opportunities to have a personal moment with me and say something that let me know that she saw me, she loved me, and she believed in me. She would take my chin into her fingertips, look me in my eyes, and say, "I love you, Child."

She poked fun at me occasionally with my teammates (about how air headed I was when I first joined the team). But ultimately, I learned a lot of life lessons just from being in her presence and wanting to live up to her expectations. She would occasionally remind us that, although we only had six team members, we were as good as all the bigger teams, and we believed her. We won superior ratings at every competition we ever entered, and we entered lots of them. Her visions were coming to pass.

The summer before my sophomore year, we had gone through a second summer dance camp to prepare for our second season as a drill team. The company that she hired this time was called The American All-Star Dance Team. They were not a local company, and we couldn't afford to travel to them. So, they sent a representative to Wilkinson County to lodge with Mrs. Hinton in her home for the entire week of camp. Because of our affiliation with this company, real opportunities started opening up for us.

In January of 1994, after two seasons under Mrs. Hinton's tutelage, she shared news that was evidence of her BIG vision manifesting. She told us that our entire drill team would be performing at the Pregame Show of Super Bowl 28 in Atlanta, Georgia. Our high school was among a few other local high school dance teams, as well as a couple of colleges that were a part of the Atlanta University Center, such as Spelman College and Clark Atlanta University.

I went from never going to Atlanta to leaving school early every day, riding a little yellow van with my teammates to go to practice in Atlanta!! It was literally a mind-blowing experience to be in a hotel conference room practicing with college girls from Spelman College. I admired them from a distance thinking, I want to be a Spelman girl one day. They looked sophisticated, well-groomed, smart, and sexy all at the same time. The way they moved. The way they focused. I just couldn't believe I was there with them.

On the day of the show, we were out on the football field rehearsing for the presentation of the Star-Spangled Banner with the legendary Natalie Cole. This alone was enough for me to die and go to heaven. I had grown up listening to her greatest hits and memorizing them all. Our assignment during the National Anthem was to hold the props, which were red, white, and blue. While Natalie Cole was singing, we were holding our props over our heads to form an aerial view of the American Flag. It was a simple job, but very important and quite an honor.

The fun part came when we were dancing on the field. The liveliest performance of the Pre-Game Show was performed by the hottest rap duo of the year, an Atlanta act by the name of Kris Kross. They were a trendy duo produced by up-and-coming producer, Jermaine Dupri. They wore extremely baggy clothing, and they really stood out because they wore some of their garments backwards. Their smash hit, "Jump" propelled Atlanta to the forefront of Black music, and everybody was feeling the new swag. So, when they performed, we really put our all into it. There were over 300 dancers on the field "jumping" around and loving every minute of it.

Then, the Charlie Daniels Band came out and performed. We choreographed for their performance, as well. However, I didn't really know who they were, so I barely remember anything about the routine. I do remember that the song was called, "The Devil Went Down to Georgia." Other people seemed to really know who they were, so I assumed that they were a big deal.

There was another moment that I will never forget. Before the Pre-Game show, we had a dress rehearsal on the field. The rehearsal required us to go out onto the field while the two football teams were warming up. (The Dallas Cowboys were playing the Buffalo Bills.) Because my younger brother was an avid student of football, I recognized a couple of those guys when I saw them. I was standing, not far at all, from Michael Irving, and I have never forgotten that. I was literally speechless. I don't think I even pointed him out to the other girls at that moment because they wouldn't have known who he was. I stared in utter disbelief. Emmitt Smith, legendary Dallas running-back, was just a few more steps away. I couldn't wait to tell my brother about it because I knew quite a bit about Smith's record-setting statistics. My brother had read books about him and others. So, he would ramble off their stats around the house.

I say all this to say, although we were from a remote town in Georgia (that no one had ever heard of) our coach had a vision for us. She wrote her goals down, and she shared her vision with us. She spoke it boldly into the atmosphere. She believed in God and us. No vision is or ever was too big for God. He is willing to blow our minds.

A year later, I was selected by The American All-Star Dance Team (the same company that connected us to the Super Bowl) to travel to Europe on a 7-Day dance tour with over 300 other girls from the United States. There was a write-up about it in the local newspaper, and my mother was so proud of me. The trip was going to cost our family around $2000, so my mother, my other visionary, went into action for me.

At the time, my mother was a dispatcher at the local Sheriff's Department. I don't know how much money she was making, but I know that it had to be very difficult to raise money for the trip. My father was working, as he had always done. I later found out that a couple of times, my mother used her whole paycheck towards my trip to Europe. I didn't know it back then.

In crunch time, though, she recruited my very loving aunt, Deborah, to help cook and sell dinners to raise the money that was left to pay for the trip. Mind you, my cousin (the same one who made the cheer team in 8th grade) was selected to go on the trip, as well. She had given up cheering and joined me on the dance team our junior year. Our flight to Europe was full of teenage girls all wearing the same sweater - red, white, and blue, stars and stripes - "American All-Star Dance Team."

My cousin was very glad that she left cheerleading behind for the drill team because we had a blast in Europe. It was the opportunity of a lifetime. My mother's vision for me was working together with my coach's vision for our team. My talents and hard work were taking me places, just as my mother had envisioned. This just shows us that it does not matter where you're from or what your background looks like. When you have a vision combined with faith and hard work, God will bring the people and opportunities to you, no matter where you are in the world.

Before we go any further:
What visions do you have for yourself?

_____
_____
_____
_____
_____

_____
Who are the visionaries who have helped to drive your success?
_____

Chapter 3

The Gift that Keeps On Giving

Prior to 2018, whenever someone would ask me who I was or what I wanted to do with my life (before age 40), I always thought of the talented singer in me. I would revert to the little girl who dreamed of being an accomplished singer, songwriter, dancer, and actress. I knew, even as a child, that it was most beneficial to be versatile, a *triple-threat* in the entertainment industry. I knew that versatility ultimately led to longevity and a strong legacy. Life was emphatically all about the performing arts in my heart and soul. Any other existence was too normal, average, unremarkable - a way of life for people who didn't have talent like mine. That's what I arrogantly thought at the time.

However, it wasn't until the Spring of 2018 that I came to understand that my gifts and talents were much more diversified than the performing arts. My heart had been transfixed on a particular vision of success for so long that I had placed a meager price tag on every other talent that I possessed.

For instance, I didn't fully appreciate the life that I'd cultivated as an established educator, a loyal wife, and a dedicated mother. I felt like I was settling for mediocrity in those roles, because there was no glitz, glamor, fame, or fortune in my routine. My predominant mindset was one that affirmed my destiny, which was, of course, global impact. So, surely this common lifestyle would not be my reality for long. Someone who could sing like me couldn't possibly be satisfied in this *ordinary* scenario. Could they?

Be that as it may, when God started closing doors in certain areas and opening doors in others, I began to understand that, sometimes, our most glorified attributes are not necessarily our most useful gifts. I reluctantly realized that just because my singing voice was the first gift, to my memory, that was strongly validated by others, it didn't define me or my purpose in life. As a matter of fact, if I look back over my life, I realize that I was a smart kid, a gifted reader and speller, well before my singing voice was discovered.

I was inquisitive and communicative from the very start. So, the talent that I thought would be my golden ticket (singing) never lost its value, but amazingly, it was rivaled by a few other serviceable gifts that God had been honing throughout my entire life. Surprisingly, these more practical abilities (communicating, asking questions, connecting with people) penetrated just as many hearts as my singing voice.

I have always enjoyed communicating with people and understanding the emotional and spiritual intricacies of what makes people who they are. I ask questions, and usually, I get answers from even the most guarded individuals. People tend to tell me things that they have never shared with anyone, which can be a huge responsibility. These heavy conversations are often very much needed and are ultimately very advantageous to both them and me.

After years of teaching adolescents - playing the role of teacher, mother, counselor, and nurse, my ability to connect with the human spirit was being activated every day, as needed.

I would listen and put myself in their shoes for a while. Then, I would share relatable experiences from my life or the experiences of others that I knew personally. But most importantly, I would give them a sense of hope. I would make them aware of the light that I saw in them, the light that God had selectively placed in each one of them - whatever light that may be. Over time, I became more and more comfortable ministering to people on the job. Children, as well as adults, showed gratitude for my listening ear, good advice, and my ability to motivate them. So, I began to realize that it was my assignment.

At first, I didn't think much of what I was doing because I was just being authentic. It's who I am, and it's quintessentially what I do. But it's not that easy for everyone, and that's why I now know that it's a gift. After 20 years of impacting the lives of adolescent children in church and community programs, I was starting to feel like I had more to offer than what I had originally perceived. My purpose was becoming clearer with each profound encounter.

When I was a senior at Wesleyan College, a private women's college in Macon, Georgia, and the first college in the world established for women, I was going through some spiritual changes. God was working on me from the inside out. He was allowing me to experience the difference between what it felt like to use my gifts for Him versus using them without a purpose.

When I first arrived on campus, I was still Shana, the singer and dancer from high school. After a few months on campus, I started to hear about a Gospel Choir that was a part of the Black Student Alliance. Although I had grown up singing in the choir, I didn't think I would fit in with the girls in the BSA Gospel Choir. They seemed sanctified and conservative. So, every time I was approached to come to a rehearsal, I politely declined the invitation. Although I was being summoned by girls who I knew were relatable, I couldn't see myself being a part of it.

Many of the members wore dresses every day with little doilies which communicated some type of religious symbolism. Unexposed, I did not understand it at all. However, after some probing from my friends, Travia Fairfax and Azania McRae, I went to rehearsal one day. Surprisingly, I walked into the most edifying environment that I had ever entered. Young ladies were on fire for Jesus, reigning over their own rehearsals, praying, testifying, and praising. They encouraged each choir member to get involved in the circle of testimonies, which was new to me. Testifying and praying in front of peers were life-changing experiences for me. It gave me a better understanding of the goal, that I was supposed to have a personal relationship with God and walk in my own faith.

So, from there, I began to seek opportunities to witness God working in my life so that I could share my testimonies. The choir became an essential part of my college experience and spiritual journey. I was quickly promoted to a leadership role as the Soprano section leader. I was very reserved in many areas of spirituality, and it was unusual to see myself growing in the ministry in God's time.

However, the choir was very anointed, and I was an important part of that. The feeling that it gave me was more fulfilling than any feeling that I had experienced when writing and recording secular music as a teenager. After a few months, I told my cousin, who was the other half of my R&B singing duet, that I was having a change of heart and I believed that I was going to use my talents for Gospel music only. When I told her this, she was reluctant to get on board with it. She expressed that she wasn't sure about the idea.

I began to start listening to Gospel artists like Yolanda Adams, who was new on the national scene at the time. My focus changed, and I was sure about this new thing. Although I was sure, I was uncomfortable talking about it with others because they didn't seem to understand why I would want to sing Gospel after recording a whole R&B album. With a humble conviction, I stuck with my gut on the decision. Although there was no recording for a while, there was a lot of growth.

  It was my last semester when God started allowing me to confirm other talents that were useful to Him. I remember encounters on the quad a few afternoons in the Spring - conversations held in the cafeteria and in the rocking chairs right outside of Porter Students Center and Burden Parlor on the beautiful Wesleyan campus. These encounters called attention to an intrinsic value that I possessed outside of singing.

Several times a week, I found myself engaging in deeply personal, confidential conversations with young ladies on campus. The young ladies were finding themselves talking to me about things that they did not intend to delve into because they barely knew me. Each time, they would say something like, "I don't know why I'm telling you this, but I feel like I can trust you."

After about the third time that this happened in one week, I began to take notice of it and realize that there might be something to what I was seeing, hearing, and feeling in these situations. The responsibility of it frightened me. I didn't understand why they trusted me with their thoughts, feelings, and secrets. I wasn't sure that I was worthy of the trust.

Then, one afternoon, I ended up casually talking with the campus police officer who was also a minister in Macon, Georgia. He had been on campus the entire four years that I was there. However, we had never spoken before. I had seen him engage in light-hearted conversations with other girls. For some reason, though, he'd never acknowledged my presence. As a matter of fact, I felt like he didn't like something about me, so I never acknowledged his presence either. Sometimes, I can be very proud in that way.

Contrary to how I'd felt about him in the past, that day was altogether different. Our conversation started with 3 people but ended with just the two of us. He ultimately talked to me about deeply personal things and told me what he saw in me as a listener. He said, "You are very easy to talk to, and that's a special gift. You could be the next Oprah Winfrey." He had no idea what he did for me at that moment. What he saw in me confirmed that my expressive personality and inquisitive nature were purposeful assets that would be used for the good of others.

Those gifts served God well when I was called into a long-term career as a public-school teacher. So, although my singing voice was the gift that I cherished the most, I realized that my ability to connect with people was the gift that kept on giving.

Before we go any further:

Has God revealed your special gifts to you?

_____
_____
_____
_____
_____

Which gifts do you think are more useful to God, and why?

_____
_____
_____
_____

Chapter 4
The Prophecy

When I graduated from college in 2000, I felt accomplished but heartbroken. I had accomplished something no one else in my family had accomplished, and I finished it with my cousin, who was more like my sister.

My grief stemmed from knowing that my old relationship was ending. All I knew was him. But something was happening mentally and spiritually, and only God would be able to help him.

So, as I walked across the stage at the prestigious Wesleyan College in May of 2000, I realized that I would have to make a big move. I needed to relocate far, far away from him to do what was best for me. But what would I do? Where would I go?

So, I applied to the At Marah School of Dance in Philadelphia, and I was accepted in July of 2000. I was so excited. The school is probably not even in existence anymore. But, at the time, I needed an extension of college, the performing arts, an opportunity to continue doing what I loved. And I needed to put space between me and this old relationship.

My cousin, Charelle, lived in Philadelphia. She was a very independent, hard-working mother of two. She was a singer, as well, so she believed in my future as an entertainer. She adamantly offered me the opportunity to come stay with her and see if we could find me a job there and network in the music industry.

I was so excited, but my parents were not. They were extremely protective, and they were hesitant to allow me to venture out, although they did encourage me to end the old relationship; Not because they did not like the young man, but because we couldn't help him. They didn't want me to be held hostage in a situation that wasn't beneficial for me.

So, their counter argument was that my cousin was too young. Therefore, I didn't need to move to Philadelphia and be a burden upon her. So, they suggested that I venture to New York with my great-aunts instead. They were older and had already helped other family members from Georgia in the past. So, I jumped on the idea! My dad called my Aunt Inez in Brooklyn and set up the plans for me to head to New York City!

By August, I couldn't believe this was working out the way it was. I was 22 years old, fresh out of college, no kids, no husband, and I was headed to New York City to make my dreams a reality!

I wouldn't have to stress over rent or anything. So, I looked at the prices of flights to New York City. They were unaffordable for me. But I didn't give up or hesitate to find other options. I had very little money, so I immediately looked at train tickets. I had always wanted to experience a passenger train anyway. Fortunately, I found a ticket to New York City for a meager $80 and purchased it right away!

I remember driving my aunt around the city, once she taught me the do's and don'ts of how-to drive in New York City. We often drove out to Far Rockaway to visit her sister, Aunt Beulah. We would collect rent from Aunt Inez's tenants. We would also frequent the bakeries and by all kinds of discounted pastries. I drove her wherever she wanted to go because she was 74 years old, and it was the least I could do.

She told me family stories, and so did Aunt Beulah. Aunt Beulah had the most nostalgic photo albums. She also cooked the best fried chicken! But anyway, I went to church one Sunday with her granddaughter, Sheena. There, I met Sheena's neighbor, who was also a musician and producer. He recorded one of my original songs for me. That was very cool. The song was a spiritual song called "What a Revelation." I had written it in college. It was my first solo recording.

So, I had been there a few weeks, and I was realizing that I was hundreds of miles away from my old relationship, and it was becoming difficult. I had spoken to him on the phone a couple of times. But when my cousin called me and told me that he was progressively getting worse in his mental decline, I cried woefully because I knew that it was over for real.

On those sad, lonely days, I would take advantage of being in a mecca like New York City. I'd walk to the Brooklyn Public Library, which looked like a museum to me. I'd try new food from one of the authentic foreign restaurants on Flatbush Avenue. My favorites were the Cuban restaurants and the Jamaican restaurants. The best element was they were within walking distance of Aunt Inez's house. I could explore it all by myself.

One Sunday, while I was still mourning the loss of my relationship, my aunt asked me to drive her to church. So, of course I said yes. She was clearly excited about me visiting her church, but I didn't know what to expect.

It was a vibrant church with a sizable turnout. However, the lead pastor did not speak that day. There was a guest speaker, which makes this encounter even less coincidental. After the guest speaker was done preaching, he pointed me out in the crowd and said "Stand up, Young Lady…. There is an old relationship that you need to let go of; Something new and better is coming, and it's going to be soooo good!"

I looked around me thinking surely, he did not just speak to my situation like that. No one had ever prophesied to me before. So, it hit me like a bus. My aunt heard it and knew exactly what he was referring to. So, from that moment, I slowly began let go and thank God for new beginnings.

A few days later, while sitting out on the stoop, I had a rare experience for a small-town girl. I saw a Mercedes pull up a couple of doors down in front of another beautiful brownstone. A young man got out and went inside the house. I knew who it was because I had been hearing about Inga and her brother from my cousins.

Inga grew up with my cousins in Brooklyn. So, to them she was still Inga. To me and the rest of the world, she was the feisty, platinum-selling, female rapper, and sidekick to rapper Jay-Z. Her stage name was Foxy Brown. I knew that her mother was next door, and I knew that her brother, who was also her manager, was in and out periodically. However, I had not seen her for myself.

There was a corner store near my aunt's brownstone. A few days later, my aunt spotted Inga leaving the corner store and heading back towards her mom's house. So, she called her over to us. Inga was so excited to see her. She even called her Aunt Inez, just like me. She was dressed down. No makeup, no lashes. No weave. No lipstick.

So, Aunt Inez said, "I Want you to meet my niece, Shana. She's from Georgia, and she just graduated from college. She sings and writes songs. I told her I wanted her to meet you." So, Inga warmly reached out to hug me, saying, "Hi, Shana. It's so nice to meet you." Her accent was so Brooklyn-ish, and I felt so un-cool when I heard her speak. Surprisingly, she was sweet. She seemed nothing like her public persona.

So, I naturally responded by saying, "Hey. How are you? It's nice to meet you, too." She literally melted as she said, "Oh my God. Your accent is so beautiful."

I humbly said, "Thank you." No one had ever said anything like that to me before. So, I said, "MY accent is beautiful?"

She said, "Absolutely, your southern accent."
Then, she told Aunt Inez that she would be sure to get with me soon, and she went inside the house.

It was unfortunate that she wasn't doing the hiring for my job interviews in Manhattan. The public relations industry had no appreciation for my southern accent at all. It was too southern for their markets. So, I quickly changed my focus from public relations jobs to Education. I also decided that I was going to go back home and start fresh. That way, I could be at my brother's football and basketball games during his senior year. I had already missed the first few games from August to November. It was time to go. So, I thanked everybody and headed South again.

    A year passed by, and I adjusted to being back home. I delved into the field of education, but I moved cautiously on the dating scene. Then, on Christmas Day in 2001, I remember my mom giving me a very beautiful sweater as a gift. I remember getting dressed after she and my dad went next door to my grandmother's house. We had made plans to go to my aunt Cookie's house for Christmas dinner. She invited us to her home in Milledgeville because it would be her last Christmas in Georgia. She was remarrying and moving to the Charleston, South Carolina area.

So, as I was getting dressed, I was walking around singing "All I want for Christmas is love" in the melody of Mariah Carey's classic song; but Mariah's lyrics were a little different. I felt in my heart that God was going to bless me with true love for Christmas.

So, after Christmas dinner, my cousin, Tasha, urged Kima and me to go to a new bar in downtown Milledgeville. She convinced us by emphasizing that it would be a long time before we would get to hang out again. I really didn't want to go out to a bar, but I reluctantly went. To make a long story short, I met someone very special that night.

He had already noticed me, but he thought I was too young for him. Subsequently, my cousin, Kima, noticed him. Instead of her considering him for herself, she said, "Shana, that guy is cute, and he's tall." We had seen so many short guys that night that it was a running joke by then.

So, she approached him and said, "My cousin wants to dance with you." So, he looked at me agreeably and nodded his head. Then, he started moving out to the dance floor. So, I met him there. He made immediate eye contact with me and said, "Why didn't you approach me for yourself?"

Our conversation flowed unusually smoothly. He was so easy to talk to. He told me he was in his last semester of college in South Carolina. So, he was only home for Christmas. I said, ok. Not bad. One semester left…

He was a year older than me, so he was the perfect age for me. I told him that I would be going to Boston over the summer to work on my master's degree at Cambridge College. He proceeded to tell me that his mother was also a teacher, and she had gotten her master's degree 30 years earlier. I initially thought he was trying to impress me because he also said he was a recording artist like me. All this compatibility was being revealed right on the dance floor in our very first conversation.

I asked him if he had any kids. He said no. So, we approvingly smiled at each other and continued to dance until the vibe of the music changed. Then, we separated. But I knew that he would find his way back to me before the night was over.

I interacted with my cousins for a while, but I kept my eye on him silently. I saw other females approaching him. But each time, he greeted them and kept it moving. After a while, I felt somebody walk up behind me and wrap their right arm around my waist. I looked around, and it was him. So, we danced until there was a ruckus that ran everybody out of the bar.

He came to see me two days later because my family buried my paternal grandfather the very next day. Then, he went back to South Carolina where he told his roommate that he had met the woman who would carry his seed. He began to come visit me on weekends while he was finishing up school. I found out a few weeks later that he was a Gordy, as in Berry Gordy and Motown Records. I asked him why he didn't tell me that part. He said, "That's not something I just go around telling people."

His grandfather and Berry Gordy were first cousins. They are a family of legacy, strong traditions, hard-work, business, education, class, and closeness. When we got married a year and a half later, our families joined together beautifully. We had our first princess a few months later, and we have been blessed to have four beautiful children after 20 years of marriage.

Although we have gone through some major trials, we have experienced immeasurable triumphs together. So, when the minister in New York prophesied that *"something new and better was coming,"* he was so right.

When God wants to get a prophesy to you, He will put the right people in the right places to make sure that you know it's coming from Him. It is not a coincidence. My husband and his family have been a blessing to my life. In Volume 2, I will share some trials and illustrate how God got us through them.

Before we go any further:

Have you ever been afraid of an inevitable change?
Share.
_____
_____
_____
_____
_____

Have you ever had a stranger to prophesy to you?
Share.

_____
_____
_____
_____
_____

Did you ever see the prophecy manifest itself?

_____
_____
_____
_____
_____

Have you ever spoken something into existence? Share.

_____
_____
_____
_____
_____

Chapter 5

Success v. Failure

Just like beauty, success is in the eye of the beholder. What looks like success to one person may not equal success at all to another person. Because of this, it's very important that we not compare our journey to anyone else's. Not just because they may have a different set of goals from our own, but also because what God has for them is for them and no one else. I think it's an unnecessary burden that we carry when we go through life competing with others, especially in our careers and other areas of life that require great commitment.

In many cases, our definition of success is influenced by our previous life experiences, such as where we come from, and what we want to experience in the future. If one person comes from a whole family of police officers, they may think it's common to become a police officer. Therefore, they may dream of being a lawyer or doctor. On the other hand, if another person comes from a family where many people have been to prison and been addicted to drugs, becoming a police officer might feel and look like a huge accomplishment. It may be the breaking of a cycle within their family, which ultimately is a huge success.

I have been a schoolteacher for 21 years. I have 3 college degrees as well as a year and a half of law school under my belt. Many people would see me as a successful person because I was the first college graduate in my immediate family on my mother's side to walk across a stage and graduate from college. I was the second on my father's side.

I felt pretty good about all these things. However, my idea of success from an early age involved music, wealth, global impact, travel, influence, etc. My teaching career did not provide any of those things. From other people's perspectives, I was successful. But it wasn't until I was older and wiser that I began to see that I was successful and protected under the Holy providence of God in the field of education.

I realized that in the eyes of God, I was successful because I was doing what He intended for me to do. He had opened the doors of education for me intentionally. He had plans for me to go into his schools and minister to young people for his purposes. I did that. So, in His eyes, I was a success. Once I submitted my will to God's will, I realized that I was a successful person because I had spent my entire adult life doing His will in my career, instead of forcing my own will upon my life. Obedience is better than sacrifice. So, we are always blessed abundantly for being obedient. 1 Samuel 15:22 states, *""Has the Lord as great a delight in burnt offerings and sacrifices as in obeying the voice of the Lord? Behold, to obey is better than sacrifice, and to listen is better than the fat of rams."*

I did not aim to become a teacher. However, every door that He ever opened for me was a door that led me into the field of education and into the lives of children. While I was in college, I was hired by the counselor of my middle school to work at the middle school's summer program for at-risk students. This was the first time I was exposed to how rewarding it was to make an impact on the lives of young people. I loved it and worked there for 3 summers.

After college, I moved to New York City with my great-aunt in pursuit of opportunities in music and media. I interviewed for jobs in media and public relations. No one hired me because of my very distinct southern accent.

But one day when I was supposed to be helping an art teacher (my friend's mom) clean up her classroom at Public School 32 in Brooklyn, the director of the after-school program came in and offered me a job teaching inner-city second graders. I did that for a couple of months before I decided to return home to Georgia.

Well, once I got back to Georgia, my aunt called me and told me that the school district needed substitute teachers every day. I called the school and inquired about becoming a substitute teacher at the middle school. They immediately placed me in a position that required me to be the teacher's aide for two whole weeks in one classroom with hearing-impaired students. By the end of the two weeks, the principal asked me if I would stay for the rest of the year as the teacher's aide. I agreed because I enjoyed it.

As the school year was nearing the end, the principal came back to me and asked me if I would be interested in having my own classroom the following year. He offered me a job as a reading teacher and cheerleading coach. I have been teaching school and involved with extracurricular activities pertaining to performing arts and sports since then.

I said all of that to say this: When we have an open, relaxed heart and submit our will to God, He will direct our path. We must recognize when He is working things out in our favor and when He is showing us the way. We can't fight his perfect will for our lives. We may not be thrilled about His will for our lives, but when we accept it wholeheartedly and find joy and fulfillment in it, He blesses us with abundance and joy in exchange for our obedience. So, I have learned that success is relative and subjective. For me, success is based upon how close I can get to executing God's perfect will for my life.

Before we go any further:

What does success and happiness look and feel like to you, if you do not consider what other people have to say about your life?

_____
_____
_____
_____
_____
_____

Chapter 6

Childish Things

Just like everybody else, I have experienced certain childhood traumas that have lingered and internalized. Unfortunately, sometimes the things we experience as young people tarnish our self-image and damage our self-confidence. Depending on how deep the wounds are, the effects of the damage can range greatly. Fortunately for me, I was raised in a relatively healthy family environment. However, I have struggled with insecurities that have hindered me, and only God gave me an avenue to overcome them and reach my full potential.

I believe that my insecurities are connected to my mother's insecurities. I have heard that when a woman carries a child, her feelings and emotions directly impact the baby that she is carrying. She was only 16 years old in 1978 when I was born. So, she was self-conscious and ashamed, which explains why I came into the world feeling self-conscious and insecure. I've spent most of my life seeking validation and wanting to prove that I am not a mistake. Although I know that my parents are proud of the daughter they have raised, it has taken me a long time to know that for myself.

Throughout my life, I have wanted to hear certain words of validation from certain people. Particularly, hearing words of approval from my parents really drove every aspect of my life. When I didn't hear the words, I needed to hear, I would equate this void to a lack of love from them or anyone, really. It was very difficult for me to receive criticism from others because I received it too harshly. My mother had been telling me that I was too sensitive all my life. So, I took that as a lack of sensitivity on her part. I tried for years to talk this issue out with others, but it always seemed to linger.

Then, in 2012, I was working on a Gospel album with my husband. He had partially produced a track and asked me to take a listen. As usual, I listened to the track and began to create a melody, which later led to lyrics. And for whatever reason, the song ended up being about everything that I just described to you - Childhood insecurities that stunt your growth and handicap you along your journey.

The song casts down the notion that other human beings can validate us when God is our creator. It even overrides the notion that we need our parents' approval. We should seek the approval of God alone and have confidence in that. He is the one who gives us self-love and internal peace. I named the song, "Childish Things, "but we never fully completed its recording.

Childish Things
by Shana Stephens

Time to put away the childish things
No more pain and insecurities
No more grudges weighing down on me
I know forgiving you will set me free

Wasting my time
Spent most of my life
Feeling unworthy and crying inside
Looking for love
From somebody else
I didn't even know how to love myself
Waiting for you to validate me
As if it were you who created me
But now I know love
Now I have confidence

*He's given me peace
And I have love within
My spirit is free
He loves me in spite of me*

*Time to put away the childish things
No more pain and insecurities
No more grudges weighing down on me
I know forgiving you will set me free*

*It's time to let go
Cause life is too short
For somebody else to control who you are
He's placed it in you
To be all you can
You can't find your value in other humans
God's in control
He's destined for you
To do all the things that he's called you to do
And you will know love
You will have confidence
He'll set you free
I know 'cause He did it for me*

*God is the best thing
 that's ever happened to me
Yeah, God is the best thing
 that's ever happened to me*

So, as we continued to work on the Gospel album, this song was pushed to the back burner because I wanted to revamp the sounds on the production and make it more up to date. Then, in 2020, a dear friend of mine launched her Christian podcast entitled *"Into the Deep."* She invited me to be an early-featured guest to speak about Education and how it is very important within a ministry. However, she also asked me to go a step further and sing a song.

So, my spirit was leading me to sing the song, *"Childish Things,"* and ask someone to accompany me on piano. So, I asked my neighbor, Alyson, with whom I had a very special musical bond. I'm so glad I asked her because when I did, she learned the song quickly, and her husband, Chris, pulled out the high-tech microphone, camera, lights, everything we needed to get a clear sound and a vivid recording of us at the piano singing.

    To make a long story short, the live, acoustic recording of the song turned out beautifully. I preferred that version of the song over the digitally produced version that we had never fully completed. I'm so glad that I stepped outside of my comfort zone and asked my friend to learn the song and play it on the piano. The Scripture says, *"Ask and it will be given to you; seek and you will find; knock and the door will be opened to you."* This masterpiece was proof of the potential that I have if I follow divine instruction and ask for the help that is already around me.

    When I submitted the song to my friend for the podcast, her response was all the validation that I needed. She told me that it ministered to her all by itself. Then, two years later, she asked me to sing the song at her women's retreat called *"Launch and Build."* The retreat was for women who were new in the ministry and were preparing to launch businesses and ministries of various kinds. The women there told me that the song felt like it was about them, and the song helped them to begin a healing process. Even my female middle school students were drawn to its lyrics and thanked me for writing and sharing the song.

Corinthians 13:11 says, *"When I was a child, I spoke as a child, I understood as a child, I thought as a child: but when I became a man, I put away childish things."* So, as we mature in Christ, we must put our childish inhibitions to the side in order that we might do His work and glorify Him despite ourselves. Instead of allowing the pains of our past to leave us bitter, we should use them to make us better.

Before we go any further:

What childhood trauma have you used for your good?

_____
_____
_____
_____
_____
_____

Chapter 7

Extraordinary Living

As I mentioned before, I had adamantly seen myself as a singer and songwriter forever. However, I knew that there was much more to ministry than just singing, so I had quietly hoped that God would strengthen other skills in me so that I could offer more than just my singing voice. I didn't see myself as a "preacher" in the traditional sense, though. I didn't have a booming voice or the propensity to preach hard like what I'd heard in the Baptist church all my life. So, I knew that it would take some time and patience for God to get me ready for His use.

In the fall of 2018, the Lord kept me up late one night in McKinney, Texas. He started flooding my spirit with ideas that would lead me into my ministry. He reminded me that not only was I gifted at singing and songwriting, but also at connecting with people and exhorting them. He showed me how He was going to give me a platform that would allow me to exhort, inspire, connect, and educate - all the things that I live for doing. He said that I was to create a YouTube Channel and call it "Extraordinary Living with Shana Stephens."

He allowed me to see a limitless vision that would be steered by His instruction and my obedience. He gave me the vision of highlighting regular people who choose to use their time, gifts and talents for good. He showed me that I would interview them, tell their stories, and inspire others to follow their examples. This idea excited me because I love getting to know people and understanding what motivates them.

The only problem was, who would I interview? I didn't know a lot of people. He assured me that everything I needed, I already had, and I already had everything I would need. He showed me where the people were already in my inner circle, and all I had to do was ask them for an interview. He began to give me the names and the questions for each interview. I grabbed a pen and wrote down the name of the ministry he gave me, the names of the people to interview, and the topics of discussion. Then, I wrote down some deadlines so that I could hold myself accountable to getting started.

The next day, I created a YouTube Channel and a Facebook page for the ministry. I began scheduling interviews, filming them, and posting them. Everybody that I reached out to was excited and helpful. God was all amid what I was putting together.

Sometimes it was discouraging, though, when the people that I knew personally would not even take the time to watch my very inspirational videos. I realized that building the following was not going to be easy. I was primarily posting the videos on Facebook and YouTube. Then, two young people whose opinions I value (Kamilah Whipple and Keandra Lewis) suggested that I consider posting my reels on Instagram where the audience is broader, and fewer people would personally know who I am. They told me that the reception would be better than Facebook where I interacted with mostly family members and friends who did not believe in my ministry, or they did not wholeheartedly support it.

So, I thought this was a great idea, but I was still a little intimidated by the idea of entering into the world of IG.

Obediently, I went ahead and uploaded all of my recorded videos onto IG under the name of @extraordinarylivingwithshana. Later, I changed my Facebook settings so that anything I posted on Facebook would automatically be posted on Instagram. However, I rarely ever clicked on the Instagram icon on my phone. It wasn't until 2023 that God was ready for me to elevate my ministry, after I had committed my heart and soul to listening for divine instruction and being obedient to it.

On January 16, 2023, Dr. King Day, I noticed that without engaging with IG, the Lord had been building a following for me there. I had almost 800 followers without knowing it. I was dumbfounded. There I was, working and wishing for support and acknowledgment on Facebook, while Instagram was hungry for what I had to offer. I posted a reel entitled "Honoring the Innocent" on Dr. King Day. Within 3 weeks, this video had over 23,000 views, 1800 likes, and 1800 shares. I knew that God was doing something different in my ministry, and I was going to make sure that I did my part by being obedient to divine instruction. I was ready for where He was getting ready to take me.

Even in the Bible, it tells the story of how Jesus had to leave his home in Nazareth at the beginning of His ministry for His works to be done in God's people. Matthew 4: 23-25 says, *"23 And he went throughout Galilee, teaching in their synagogues and proclaiming the gospel of the kingdom and healing every disease and every affliction among the people. 24 So his fame spread throughout all Syria, and they brought him all the sick, those afflicted with various diseases and pains, those oppressed by demons, those having seizures, and paralytics, and he healed them. 25 And great crowds followed him from Galilee and the Decapolis, and from Jerusalem and Judea, and from beyond the Jordan."*

Sometimes, for us to be used by God, we must go amongst strangers who are not familiar with us. So, I changed my social media focus from Facebook to both Instagram and TikTok. God basically told me to not give up on my ministry, but to cast my nets on the other side in an unfamiliar land. From there, *Extraordinary Living* grew steadily. It has allowed me to use all of my gifts and talents, to be myself, just as God intended me to be.

Before we go any further:

Write down a time when God gave you an assignment and he provided everything you needed because of your obedience.

_____
_____
_____
_____

_____

Chapter 8

If Not You, Then Who?

In 1949, my family was struck by tragedy in the most traumatic way when my grandmother's oldest brother was tortured and killed by a mob of racist whites in Irwinton, Georgia. It is believed the mob was orchestrated and assisted by the Sheriff of Wilkinson County. The mob came into the small jailhouse, grabbed the keys to the cell, which were left there for them, and took my uncle from the jail cell. From there, I've been told that he was tortured, dismembered, shot in the head, and left on the side of a major Georgia highway right outside of town.

This tragedy led to a diaspora within our family. My other uncles' lives were threatened, and they were warned by whites to get out of town. So, all of my grandmother's brothers left Wilkinson County, never to live there again.

Two of my grandmother's sisters left, as well. Those siblings who left landed in New York City and Detroit, Michigan, where they settled and built successful lives for themselves and their children over the next 50-70 years until they departed from this earth. My grandmother and two sisters remained in Wilkinson County until their departures.

My first-time hearing about this heinous murder was in the early 80's when I was about 8 years old. My paternal grandfather sat on the front porch on a hot summer day and told about 5 or 6 of us about our uncle. It was a lot for us to digest, but he felt like we needed to know. My grandfather had a strong distrust toward whites, and he made it known. He and my uncle, who was his brother-in-law, had been very close.

My grandmother, Lucy Hill Underwood, everybody lovingly called her "Sweet" because she was just that. She was quiet and humble. She had a bad stutter, so she didn't talk very much. She was a homemaker and a farmer. However, I later learned from an older cousin that she was a jack of all trades, like my father and like her older brother, Caleb Hill, Jr. who was killed.

Her sister, Beulah, who moved to New York, told me that the timid, withdrawn woman that she became was a result of the trauma and the fact that she remained in the place where their brother was killed. She had once been a spunky dresser with a more outgoing personality.

When I think of my grandmother, I think of how she cooked soulful dinners and fed anybody who came to "The Bottom." However, she was a woman of few words and a woman who never ventured far away from "The Bottom."

I remember loving her immensely and thinking that she was white until I was about 5 years old. I loved her and she loved me. I loved being in her home, playing on her land, eating her food, and combing her hair. She loved me because I was her baby boy's first born, and I was undeniably just like him.

My father was only 19 years old when I was born, but my grandmother loved me dearly despite the circumstances. She loved to feed me, and I loved to eat her food. It was a treat to go visit her humble home because I was treated so specially every time I went there. I watched her work in the gardens and eventually we helped her harvest crops. Then, she would cook for us. She was the ultimate homemaker.

When I was a little older, she started to get sick and display symptoms of Alzheimer's or some form of dementia. I was a child, so I didn't know much about it. But I knew that she had a dresser covered with medications. I inherently knew that the amount of medication that she was consuming was not normal.

Over time, she slowly started to slip away from us until she became bed-ridden and unconscious of us around her. My grandmother passed away in 1994 when I was 16 years old, but it felt like we had lost her several years earlier.

It was not until I was older that I fully understood what she had endured as a very young woman. The sudden loss of her brother, the extreme grotesque nature of his murder, the agony of staying in the place where he was mutilated. The frustration and humiliation that came with the complicit disregard for his life.

Some whites were quoted in a national newspaper as saying, that he was "just a nigger." When you know that your brother was a blessing to his family, a hard-working chalk-miner, a bold entrepreneur, a landowner, a homeowner, a farmer, and a local philanthropist. He was a good-looking man who had no fear of another man of any race. That was his crime. He had the audacity to think he deserved to own a brand-new car in 1949. He had the audacity to take the Sheriff's gun when the Sheriff tried to man-handle him at the nightclub. So, because of these attributes, some supremacists felt like he deserved to die the way he did. But my grandmother knew better.

He was a provider and a family man who was already taking care of his crippled father, Caleb Hill, Sr., as well as his two youngest sisters. When he was taken away from our family, the impact was devastating. For our family, not only was there the pain of the tragic loss, but the threat of more violence if anyone spoke out against the sheriff and the other responsible parties.

J. Edgar Hoover and the FBI got involved in the case. However, the GBI, the local authorities, and local witnesses would not cooperate. So, the case was left cold for the next 70 years. When I look back over what I saw from my grandmother, she was a woman who lived in trauma, and over time, it consumed her.

Fast forward to 2022, my grandmother has been gone for 28 years. I'm 44 years old, living right outside of Dallas, Texas with my husband and our four children. A cousin of mine on the maternal side of my family reached out to me from Atlanta and told me about a TikTok that he had seen about Caleb Hill, Jr. Then, someone else told him that Caleb Hill, Jr. was a member of my family on my father's side. So, he shared the TikTok video with me.

The same cousin asked me how it was possible that he was born and raised in Wilkinson County and had never heard about this atrocity. Sadly, this was only possible because the terroristic silencing was so effective that no one in the county knew about this heinous crime except for those who were alive at the time that it took place.

When it happened, The New York Times, The Chicago Tribune, and many newspapers around the nation sent reporters to Irwinton, Georgia, but that did not work in our favor. My older family members certainly were not openly talking about it throughout my youth. However, I had recently been engulfed in research on it. So, I wanted to talk.

The TikTok reel was produced by a young man from Chicago, Illinois. He told me that he would soon be starting a new podcast with producers from Chicago, and that he would like me to possibly be his first guest. He wanted to talk about the lynching of my uncle. I agreed to do it. However, as soon as I got off the phone with him, I began to get anxious about the possible repercussions within Wilkinson County. The devil wanted to bind me before I even had a single conversation. Therefore, I could only imagine the type of fear and suppression that my grandmother and her siblings experienced in 1949 and thereafter.

So, I went home and had a glass of red wine in hopes of calming my nerves. I was upstairs in my bedroom alone. My children were in their rooms and my grandmother was on my mind very heavily. For about an hour she was there in my spirit, not letting go of my thoughts. She was telling me not to be afraid and that now is the time. She said to me, I had to be silent until the day that I died, and I need you to tell people what happened to my brother.

I was very intent on listening because I had not heard her voice in so long. I was concerned about what other family members would say and feel about me being the one to speak up about it. Then she said, "If not you, then who?" Then, I had an unforgettable, first-time experience with the Holy Spirit. God allowed me to connect with my grandmother emotionally and spiritually.

For about 15 minutes, I laid sprawled across my bed, feet on the floor with my arms outstretched on the bed. God allowed me to have an out-of-body experience in which my grandmother's spirit entered mine. He allowed me to be there with her. In 1949. In the darkness. In the pain. In fear. In loneliness. I cried out in despair, from the depths of my belly. For fifteen minutes or more, tears fell, and I hurt my grandmother. I understood her much more than ever before, and I mourned her experience profoundly.

From there, everything changed for me. My grandmother and the Holy Spirit confirmed for me that I was the one, and that I was to have no more fear. The time for fear was over. This story was going to reactivate change in the world, and my obedience was going to elevate my impact forever. I had no idea when, where, or how we were going to do it, but I knew that she and I would share the story together. To this day, my most viewed original video features him on the cover.

Before we go any further:

Can you think of a time when you were afraid to do something important, and the Holy Spirit promised to protect you?

_____
_____
_____
_____

Chapter 9

Soul Ties

I strongly believe that family members who are closely knit together share soul ties. When our spirit has been penetrated by the love and influence of family, the Holy Spirit connects us in ways that we often do not acknowledge or even realize. I was blessed to be raised by two villages. My mother's side of the family has its own village, which allowed me to have the daily influence of my parents, aunts, uncles, grandparents, and great-grandparents until they departed this earth. I played with all my first cousins every day of my childhood.

On my father's side of the family, we call our village" The Bottom." When I was growing up there, our village consisted of my grandmother, grandfather, aunts, uncles, and first cousins, as well. Many may not be able to understand a life like this. It may seem like something from a movie or a simpler place in time because it is. However, it is a very safe, rich, blessed way to grow up because you are shaped and groomed by everybody around you. Everybody feels an obligation to look out for you.

Where your parents fall short, the aunts and uncles rise to the occasion. When division threatens the village, the grandparents and great-grandparents assert their authority and apply their wisdom so that the village stays intact. Family values are instilled, enforced, and passed down from generation to generation. You are loved, protected, guided, and exhorted into becoming the best version of yourself.

To make a long story short, my aunts and uncles are additional parents for me. My cousins are equivalent to my siblings. So, the soul ties are much stronger than we ever realize. I didn't realize this until I was living a thousand miles away from my family in McKinney, Texas - right outside of Dallas. A few things happened in my spirit life that showed me how our souls are tied to our family members more than we know. God prepares us for the things that are about to happen concerning those we love and those who also love us.

My aunt, Deborah, is my mother's older sister by one year. I was born when my aunt, Deborah, was 17 years old. So, we have literally grown up together. She has been my mother's best friend her entire life, so she has helped raise me, and she has done it with genuine love. This aunt is the glue that holds our family together, now that Granny is gone. She has always enjoyed raising children, cooking, combing hair, and taking care of home. Loving her family is her superpower. She possesses the rare ability to support her nieces and nephews just like her own children.

So, in the Spring of 2019, I was 40 years old and pregnant in Texas. None of my family in Georgia knew about it at the time. One week I noticed that I kept thinking of my aunt at random times as I was listening to classic Motown music in my classroom. I was playing upbeat music as my students were doing their work, and I kept having flashbacks of times when I had seen her dance and laugh. (She has this infectious laugh that makes life better for everybody around her.)

I was reminiscing on good times to the point where I was smiling and even giggling to myself a little. I even went on social media and posted a picture of the two of us together when I was about two years old. Then, I noticed that this had happened two days in a row, so I started to become concerned about my aunt. Is she ok? Why is she in my spirit so heavily this week?

Within a couple of days, she suffered a massive stroke. This shocked everybody because she appeared to be relatively healthy. As a result, she was in a coma for several weeks, and our entire village was afraid we were going to lose her. The doctor said that she had a 3% chance to wake up from the coma. So, here I am a thousand miles away, afraid that I may lose the closest person to my mother. So, my prayer life went into overdrive. I also taught my daughters, in that moment, that God honors the prayers of children.

They jumped right into daily prayer on the way to school and every night before bed. I however, began to pray and play praise and worship music from sunup to sundown. I felt like I needed the Lord so desperately to let us have my aunt back. Just let her wake up.

Then, one night after four weeks of worrying, I had a dream about my aunt. She and I were sitting in a beauty salon together. She was sitting under one hair dryer, and I was under another. She was talking to me, and she looked fine. Her mind was sharp, and her speech was clear. She told me that she was going to be ok. She was going to live!! After about a month in a coma, she woke up with the ability to speak, write, and remember everything and everybody. She could not walk, but her beautiful mind was intact.

The Holy Spirit prepared me for her getting sick and for her waking up in her right mind. If we pay attention to our spirit man, we can be alerted of things coming for those we love. He also uses certain people to draw us into Him. My aunt is His living sacrifice. He used her to draw her family members to Him. My prayer life intensified while she was in the coma, and so did the prayer live of her other immediate family members.

In the Fall of 2020, a family feud took place on my father's side of the family. Everyone involved was deeply wounded. But what made matters worse was the fact that the whole debacle took place on social media for the world to see. The feud put me in a position where I felt like I had to stay out of it because I had always been close to everyone involved. It was one of the most heartbreaking family experiences I had ever had. So, for about a year, there were family members who were not speaking or visiting one another during the pandemic. I never thought I would see my father's family divided the way that it was.

In the fall of 2021, a year later, I had two aunts on my father's side to pass away 32 days apart. They were my father's sisters. Two very significant women in my life. Because they were the first aunts that I lost, I did not realize how deep the soul ties were until they both passed away. When the first one passed away, I had already been praying for her because she was very sick and had been battling various medical conditions for years. But she always pulled through.

    Well, that fall, I was living in Texas while the rest of my family was in Georgia. I saw some family photographs on Facebook that allowed me to see just how frail my aunt had become. In my spirit, I knew that she was possibly too frail to recover this time. A bad feeling set into my stomach. That same night, she suffered a bruising fall, which was a very painful thought. I went online and ordered some flowers for her because I knew she loved flowers.

    When she received them, she asked me to give her a call, so I did. We talked for about an hour, and she told me that the flowers meant so much to her that she cried when she received them. I knew that she and I were good, despite the lingering family issues between some others.

About a month later, I was at work on a Friday morning. I was all excited about a milestone that I had reached in my personal life. However, I was having intense pain in my back, which I found out was due to menstrual discomfort. The pain was right in the middle of my spine, right on my tailbone. I had never experienced such intense pain in my back before. I could not stand for long. I could not sit comfortably during my classes.

Then, around 1:00 in the afternoon, I decided to just sit at my desk for a little while. And during the one o'clock hour, I noticed that all my back pain unexplainably went away. Something supernatural was happening. I felt a spirit encircling me. But it was a very happy spirit. It felt like my body and soul were in perfect harmony with one another and there was no stress. Not only was there no physical pain, but there was also no emotional or spiritual worry for those few minutes. My spirit felt lifted and free from everything that had ever made me sad or worried. It felt like a cocoon of peace and joy was engulfing me, and I could do nothing but bask in the glory of it. It was a fullness that I never knew existed. It felt like heaven on Earth.

It lasted for about 10-15 minutes, then I returned to my earthly existence. I did not know what was happening to me until I arrived home after work. I received a phone call from my cousin who informed me that my aunt had passed away. The first of the two. As we continued to talk, I found out that she had passed away during the hour in which the Holy Spirit engulfed me. As a matter of fact, she passed away at almost the precise time that the spiritual cocoon was encompassing me.

    I was overwhelmed by this unexpected supernatural experience. God was taking my aunt away from me, but he blessed me to feel for just a moment what heaven was like. He reassured me that she was no longer in physical, mental, or emotional pain. She was ascending into heaven to take her rest, and she would suffer no more. When God allowed me to experience this with her, it reaffirmed the bond that I have always felt with her and my other aunts. I knew that the love was impenetrable on my end, but this experience let me know that there are soul ties between family members that physical death cannot terminate.

When I went home for her funeral, I was met with the gut-wrenching reality that my eldest aunt on my father's side had fallen gravely ill. So, when the funeral of the first aunt was over, I returned to Texas with a sickening feeling in my spirit. It warned me that I would be making the trip back home very soon. I didn't want to accept it, but the second aunt died just over 30 days later. She was the aunt who was always involved with us in the schools and the church. She was fully committed to our generation, making sure she showed us how much she believed in us and making sure we did what we were supposed to be doing to represent our school, church, and family.

When she passed away, her spirit became an influential part of my life because I felt like someone had to continue the legacy that she left behind. She was very instrumental in keeping traditions going and supporting her children, nieces, nephews, and grandchildren. She was a warrior, and I wanted to be just like her.

She inspired me just by showing me that she believed in me, and she appreciated me. She taught me so much by her example. She showed me how to tirelessly love and support others. When she died, I knew that I had to return home to serve in my home church because she poured her heart and soul into it for decades, along with my uncle. I had to do it for her. She still speaks to me from heaven, and I listen. Soul ties. They influence us both consciously and unconsciously.

So, although I hated to lose my aunts, the first aunt's transition allowed me to get a taste of heaven, which is more loving than anything she could have ever done for me in her physical form. The second aunt's support for me, her vigor for church, family, and community have provided me with direction, purpose, and spiritual fire at a time when the enemy could have used me in other ways. Romans 8:28 says "And we know that in all things, God works for the good of those who love him, who have been called according to His purpose."

Before we go any further:

Have you ever felt a soul tie with someone? Share.

Chapter 10

The Wilderness

    I never liked being alone as a child. I didn't understand the importance of silence and meditation. I grew up in a family village in a remote town where everybody knew everybody. My village consisted of my great grandparents, my grandparents, my parents, my mother's siblings, and their children. So, I grew up in a cushion of love and support.
    I grew up with the same sheltered dynamic on my father's side of the family. Our village consisted of my grandparents, my father's siblings, and their children all thriving on the family's land together. It was awesome, the way all children should grow up.

No matter where I migrated to in the southeast, I always knew that I could go to Wilkinson County, Georgia to be replenished with love and adornment from both villages. So, that's what I did all my adult life. By 2015, all my grandparents had passed away. So, I was clinging to their memories, their teachings, and their inspiration. I didn't want to lose any of it because my ancestors meant everything to me. Their dreams, their hopes, their pride, and their accomplishments.

By 2021, I had been married 18 years, and we had four beautiful daughters in metropolitan Dallas, Texas. Although my husband and I had a few issues that had been ongoing for years, something felt different around May 2021. The Holy Spirit was up to something. It warned me that our last year in Texas would be tedious and lonely.

It told me that several people were going to be moving out of my inner circle, and there was nothing I could do about it. That was the saddest feeling that I had ever felt in the spiritual realm. I remember sitting in our recording studio right next to my husband when God revealed to me that I was getting ready to enter *The Wilderness*.

So, the closer it got to my oldest daughter's high school graduation, the more I was preparing to move back home. I secured a job in Georgia 3 whole months before we moved, and school did not start until August.

I felt like there was something purposeful about me returning home, but I didn't know what. Whatever it was would be fulfilling God's will for my life. I had no clue why He was doing it. But all these things would soon be revealed to me.

So, when I finally arrived in Georgia just a few days after my daughter graduated from high school, my family's eyes lit up around me. We partied every day in some form or fashion. Surprisingly though, when I moved back home onto my family's property, God began to remove people from my inner circle in His own way. The ones who could not be a part of the journey that he was about to take me on. It was sad, disappointing, and lonely in The Wilderness because I thought I had come home to be with the ones He was removing.

To say the least, I was going through the toughest time in my life. My oldest daughter was heading off to college at Louisiana State University, 8 hours away, in just a few weeks. So, I felt like I was losing my left and right hands at the same time. I knew one thing for sure - I was in *The Wilderness*.

But anyway, we will get back to that issue later. After months of being in The Wilderness, feeling rejected, disregarded, discarded, and humiliated, I began to realize something. I'm here in this place alone in the flesh. There's nobody truly in this place with me, but God. He has never left my side. Despite the people maneuvering around me, in and out of my life, here today, gone tomorrow - He has never once forsaken me or my children.

To describe it all to you would be a book all by itself. It would take too long. So, I will just say that He proved to me that even when I'm in the wilderness, He is not only there, but He loves having my undivided attention.

I realized that He was there with me when everyone else was preoccupied, angry, lost, or untrustworthy. So, I figured since He was the only one that I could truly rely on, I should trust Him. He was faithful and true to me. He favored me when others had no interest in me and excluded me.

I decided that my goal in life would be to always follow His instruction, even when I was afraid. So, I went into 2023 with a made-up mind. I would listen to His voice and follow divine instruction. It was worth a try at 44 years old. And that's when my whole world began to change in the Spirit and subsequently in the natural realm. He placed me in The Wilderness so that He could equip me with the spiritual strength to faithfully follow His instruction.

Before we go any further:

Has God ever removed people from your life against your will? Share.

_____

_____

_____

How did He equip you in your wilderness?

Chapter 11

Obedience

I have been a Christian all my life, and I have had a personal relationship with God all my adult life. I can look back over my life and see how I have matured in stages. It's always exciting for me to witness myself growing closer to God. But I must say that the most empowering step that I have ever taken in my life is deciding to listen for divine instruction and be obedient to it. Waking up every day, knowing that I am under the direction of the one and only living God is liberating. It takes away the fear, uncertainty, and pressure of figuring it all out on my own.

    I know when God is speaking to me because I have a feeling of conviction in my spirit. It may be a still small voice, a message from another person, or Scripture. When we pray without ceasing, we become keenly aware of when God is speaking to us. Therefore, much prayer equals much power.

When we follow divine instruction, we begin to see the fruits of our labor pay off in greater dividends and in shorter periods of time. God loves to reward His obedient children, and 1 Samuel 15:22 says that *"Obedience is better than sacrifice."*

Once I started listening for God's voice and waiting on the Lord, I saw doors open in my life. I saw a change in my confidence to declare and decree things and my faith in casting down strongholds.

I saw my hands begin to heal others in the name of Jesus. There is power in the name of Jesus. Chains are broken, and mountains move. But we first must hear from Him and do everything in His name.

Before we go any further:

Are you able to hear from God? Explain.

_____

Are you committed to following divine instruction?

_____

Chapter 12

Reflections

I hope this memoir will be a beacon of light in someone's life, a testimony and an instrument of praise that pleases God. It is in my obedience that this book was completed. So, I pray that it is a blessing to whom it was intended for. When I first began to write it, I didn't feel that my story was profound enough to inspire other people. I thought that God could only use the stories of those who came from sad circumstances, such as your typical Cinderella story.

However, I learned from this experience that each one of my shared experiences stands alone as a testament to how God operates in our daily living. It's not always about a chronological series of events that tells someone's entire life story. Most of all, I have learned that if God is getting the glory, the story is worth telling someone who needs salvation, healing, redemption, or whatever the need is.

Most of all, from writing this memoir, I have learned that any time we keep God at the helm of our journey, our journey will be *extraordinary*, filled with millions and millions of little miracles. It's our choice to focus on the good around us instead of the negative. Acknowledging that God is the one holding it altogether for us is the *extraordinary* part. He is the one performing the miracles, connecting the dots, watering the roots, and making the revelations.

God gave me the name *Extraordinary Living* very vividly, but I wasn't exactly sure why in 2018. Now, I know that it's because, without God in our lives, life is ordinary. It's unfulfilling, empty, and void. He is the EXTRA. He is the ingredient that makes it worth doing every day.

He puts the smile on my face, the pep in my step, the rhythm in my rock, and the swag in my sway. I love living, and it's because I can find joy in Him every day. He fills every void and heals every heart. Acknowledging God in the little things is an extraordinary way to live.

I'm very passionate about how good God has been in my life because I am very grateful. There's so much more that I could have included in the testimonial because 2023 turned out to be the single most trying year of my life. However, I have saved some of the stories for Volume 2. So, stay on the journey with me. I love you.

Before we go any further:

Do you feel like you have a testimony worth sharing with others? Share briefly.

_____
_____
_____

FEEDBACK

Thank you so much for reading my first book and sowing into this ministry. I would really appreciate your feedback as I push forward. Please reach out to me at extraordinaryliving2018@gmail.com with the following feedback.

Email me and tell me 2 things.

A. Which testimonial *engaged* you the most as you learned more about my life? How?

_____

_____

_____

B. Which testimonials *helped* you the most in terms of your *spiritual growth*?
(Give your top 3.)

_____

_____

_____

You may sow into the ministry via Cash App at **$Extraordinary2018**

Acknowledgments

I would like to thank God for inspiring me to write this book and guiding me through the process. I would also like to thank a few people for planting the seed, too. Lavonne Smith, Apostle Claudia Johnson, Cheryl Foreman, Renee Hastings, and Charelle Greene. Thank you to Melissa Samuel for giving me the idea to make the book a devotional. Thank you to Khara Barnard for encouraging me to record the audiobook. Thank you to my parents and my immediate family for your patience and support as I pursue my goals and walk in my purpose.

Made in the USA
Columbia, SC
18 January 2024